Her

Channah Smith

BookLeaf Publishing

India | USA | UK

Presentation by *BookLeaf Publishing*

Web: www.bookleafpub.com

E-mail: info@bookleafpub.com

ISBN: 9789358313949

First edition 2023

*This is dedicated to my family and friends who
have continuously supported my poetry and
other creative ideas.*

ACKNOWLEDGEMENT

I would like to give all the honour and glory to God for making poetry my purpose and vision.

You

Narcissists like to hear sorry, when there doesn't need to be one.

Serenity

I'm never worried about the parties I'm not
invited to,
I'll take heed to where I can flourish,
I love my own company the most but don't
mistake that for me being rude,
I'm just used to the feeling of solitude.

I find it funny how people can scream 'black
lives matter' but then police black women,
and still expect to be cuffed.
Education is a must.

I'm no longer shackled to the expectations of
beauty,
I can't adhere to a standard that was never meant
for me.

I'm not worried about being a baby mother,
but rather a single mother in a marriage because
fathers simply can't manage.
Babysitting your child is delusion,
just like podcasts still asking what do women
bring to the table?
You just want to apply a label because you see
value in what a woman can do rather than a
woman can make you feel,
So I'm not trying to hear both perspectives, let's
be real.

Respecting woman has to extend beyond your
mother and your sister

It's getting light out but I'm not going to use
summer as an excuse to be a Lukewarm
Christian.
I felt cold in your presence because I felt your
absence before your departure
so despite all the laughter it echoes away in thin
waves.
I catch flights and feelings don't let this facade
get to you.
I put in the hours chasing the paper so it's
standard that I'm up in the evening.

Transition

I often wonder at what moment do you transition
into adulthood?
Is it when you're able to vote?
Or shivering outside a nightclub because you
should have brought a coat?
Or listening to the horrid song on hold, whilst
trying to arrange a doctor's appointment at 8am?
Becoming a midnight owl for a monthly
paycheck.

When I sleep late to wake up early, it becomes
habitual, time runs away from me.
This was not my idea of the circle of life, and I
worry when I will be a wife?
The ease of writing wishlists, finding time to
complete my to-do lists.
Checking emails more than social media, and
thinking I don't want to wait 3-5 business days.
I'm impatient and the world used to revolve
around me, not me around it.

But I can no longer tick under 18, I'm 21 and
over.

So I read all the fine print and the terms and conditions, and ask for a copy of everything I sign.
Sometimes I choose not to disclose my race, so I'm not discriminated against, and other times I do, so that companies can vouch for equality.

Honestly, just tip the waiters. We really have to appreciate their patience. I no longer moan about increasing the price of a bag for life, I just bring my own, because when a meal deal is no longer £3.00, Tesco's has bigger fish to fry.

TFL robs me blind at 2am a night, so it doesn't make me feel guilty for my addiction to Uber. We have a love-hate relationship, somehow it draws me back in. I do miss the beeping sound my oyster used to make, but I worried when I lost it, rehearsing how a new one was coming in 2 weeks to the Bus Driver. He still didn't let me on.

I loved being sent to the shop, because that always meant I could get myself a treat. Now the idea of food shopping, physically exhausts me. I never have a pound for the bloody trolley and I underestimate how much I can actually carry home.

I love a spontaneous 'get my life together' in the middle of the night, it's mostly followed by a deep clean along with music. Some songs are so good, I only listen to it once a week, so I don't get sick of it.

I'm unable to stick to a diet, I just eat the food I like when I feel like it. There are so many rules around food, I don't want to have an unhealthy relationship with it. What works for me, may not for you. But if you do like Marmite, I am going to have to re-evaluate my relationship to you. I love sweets, especially their variety. Liquorice appeals to the eye but once tasted it leaves behind a bitter sour taste. A bit like some men. I don't eat sweets as much but I buy wrappers for fun. I also swapped apple juice for rum, never been a smoker so the only thing I'm billing is tax.

When does becoming a 'sweet little girl' turn into 'slag' when men are hit with rejection. How do they run for election? My definition of success is no longer solely about money, but about experiences, relationships and achievements. I want to sit back and say life is good, and be proud because that's all I've ever wanted for my future. Although adulting is a strange process, I always remain in high spirits.

Never dim your light, unless it's to transfer
savings into your current account. Hermes is
defo crap but my focus is that everybody needs
to be delivered by Christ.

Fly Away

Eye contact is deadly,
     so I turned the other way,
     but you brought mystery to my
life,
     so I kept on becoming Lot's wife.

     Felt exquisite like a butterfly,
     but some of them live up to
weeks,
    so maybe we were never really playing for
keeps,
     so in the bat of an eyelid I became
a moth,
     annoying and in the way,
thinking whether I should pop up to you during
the day.

Felt like taking flights because you would air me
in plain sight.
           I was trying to be nice.
        Fighting your corners and we weren't even
in the same room,
     at some point you left.

           I didn't notice because I was in the
dark.

           Trampled all over my carpet, as if it were
a zoo,
              I wouldn't let anyone step on it,
            even if their shoes were brand new,
                  but I let you.
        It's beyond me how I let you slide like that,
                 but you're sly like that,
            got this obscure demeanor about you.

              I'm glad you sailed away,
            because all you used to do is export,
       and when I wanted more respect you used to
fall short.
            I sliced my expectations in half,
        only for you to rain on me when I needed
shade,
             I was always dreaming,
           so my perception of you became
clouded.

Maybe if I opened my window,
I could have been soft where I needed to be
for us to program.

There was a lot on my table,
so I was barely stable,
I still put you on my plate and consumed,
your time and energy,
but I put myself at jeopardy,
because now you remain a memory.
So I have to heal with a brave face
on,
and process what I had to digest

One night I cried because you were meant to
help me fly.

Perception

I used to have periods where I would uninstall
instagram, because it would feed me lies that I
was not the standard.
I wanted to take cute selfies, but I wasn't 90%
sure that they looked decent, and deleted it two
days later.
Somehow the more I look at my photos, I see a
lack of beauty, grace and femininity

I used Pinterest for inspiration, but I would have
to add Black Woman on every search, which
became so tiring.

I have compounded a folder in my camera roll of
tik-tok videos of quick workout routines on how
to remove belly fat, but would just store them.
I obsess over the appearance of myself, the
stretch marks that trail across my hips and the
scars that scatter themselves along my body
without my permission.

I always second guess skincare products, and
question if it was suitable for darker skin.
I've spent so much on skincare to accept that
hyperpigmentation is okay.

It is not the end of the world.
The girl in me screams that I just want to put on
my good clothes and play outside.
However, we're not playing with toys instead,
we're competing for likes, status, comments, and
validation.
Where Women talk about Turkey with no
reference to a Sunday.

Bigger does not mean better, and people should
be viewed as an entirety and not mechanical
parts.
I owe it to my younger self to handle myself
with care, as the content is limited edition

Both Sides

When I hear xoxo I think of Vybz kartel and you
think of gossip girl.
Nothing is wrong we're just in different worlds,
I never want people to think of me as average,
What if I don't want to chase the bag because
it's plastic?
I'm branded with the art of evolving so I can't
pick things that are prone to molding.
I gel with people who like to take up space, and
you can't if you don't let anxiety edge you on.
I'm not on what you're on, I don't want to just
do it to feel like a champion I need balance.
So I'll take my time

I've been on dating sites but I've felt so
unhinged because men wanna screw around for
fun.
I like masterchef, writing and makeup tutorials
that I have no intention of re-creating.
So when my girls are dating, I hope he
complements your life other than with money
and if not sure, ditch him, a Barbie can definitely
bank on her own.

I'm not into that struggle love.
That I can change that man kind of love.
So I may destroy you like chewing gum because
you left behind a bitter taste in my mouth.
But still I'll bounce back like a flexi rod set and
let it speak volumes even though I love
shrinkage.

The smallest things make me happy,
Like the art of existing and creation before my
eyes.
So burn your bikini body you already embody
beauty,
and black men I would rather you explain your
hurt than wear your face on a shirt.

You are loved for many of reasons which I don't
have time to explain.

So choose yourself, when the world doesn't
choose you.

15

Lover Girl

I suppose me not having access to you in the way that I want makes me feel as if I won't meet that person. I find it so weird how we are very different but alike at the same time. I've accepted that I'm a lover girl and I want to be shown that I am loved in as many ways as possible.
I want messages throughout the day that make me smile at my phone like an idiot. And reread them over again. I want unexpected flowers. Home cooked meals. Hugs under your jumper. Forehead kisses. I would say kiss in the rain but I don't want either of us to be sick the next day. Embrace me like how coco bread does with patty. Endless laughter. Sex that is not just physical.
The sharing of knowledge through deep conversation. And I'm not talking would you

rather questions. Massages that take me and you
to another dimension. Long walks that feel like
seconds, because time simply doesn't exist when
I'm with you. Loving you on the days you don't
love yourself. To know that we don't have to be
talking, yet I'm content with the sound of
silence. Holding your hand. When people see us
I want them to think we complement each other
well.

To have and to hold. I want your spirit to keep
me young. I want to play fight even though I
know the odds are against me. The optimism of
a Rastafarian with endless Proverbs to tell. For
our communication to be a two-way street, and
not just a response of 'I hear it. Because you can
understand but not comprehend. I wanna be your
friend as much as I am your person. So I want to
see both versions. I pray you like pets.
I want us to always court, but for you to never
judge me. I want your body mass to crush me,
when giving me hugs on top. I want to lie with
you knowing that we will always pick each other
back up. I want to steal your food even though I
have my own. I want home not to be a place but
wherever you are.
I'd love for God to bless this union. To keep you
in my prayers. For you to support my writing, on
the days I have no inspiration. The sound of my

name bouncing between your lips to feel like a symphony. Sing for me even if you think you're rubbish. Can I gaze into your eyes and inspect the perplexity of its form? I want to have our baby, and not just have a baby by you. I don't need to tattoo your name, because you will be on my heart. I'm not scared of love but I sometimes think it's scared of me. I only want it to happen once, so until then I will wait.

P.S Our Children are supporting Arsenal

Currently

I hate listening to songs that remind me of
people I used to associate them with.
I still don't know what love is.
Corinthians 13 says that love is kind and patient,
and then I'm reminded that people are easily
complacent.
Some things are black and white,
and I still see red,
I never like to address the things that you said.
Sometimes ignorance is bliss.

I've never been pregnant, but there has been a
miscarriage of justice for my people, because if
we're equal why are we still treading around on
thin needles.

Women get pregnant and I don't see men
around, they need to come to their senses and
stop the defensive dialogue of 'she is wrong.'
You should have kept the same energy when you
were taking off her thong.

People say things like I was born in the wrong
era or generation, but no matter what period it is,
someone always has blood on their hands, and
the cycle continues.
It's a cold world, that's why some of us have
crooked smiles, cuz the trials we go through just
mash us down.

I don't worry about the BBL, I worry about the
EDL.
Spewing out statements like 'Britain ain't like it
used to be.'
Annoyed at the man who makes kebabs,
Or the Muslim Women wearing a hijab.
I mean people need to seriously question their
sanity,
when you feel rage at seeing a Sainsbury's
Advert cast a black family.

But 'you don't see colour' so it's okay.
You really missed the point, to be blunt I want to
be seen as a Black Woman, I don't need you to

tell me you're not racist because you have black
friends, it's your views that you need to amend.

I praise and rejoice the Lord through the roof, so
it sickens me to hear that the Priests prey on the
youth.
I always tell people to live their truth.
If you are ever in the decision making process,
always ask yourself 'Am I choosing me.'

The reality is you don't really miss me, you miss
the history and I'm past learning my lesson.

Overthinker

I don't like to call loved ones when I know they
are outside, I somehow feel as if me ringing
them will be the reason for them colliding with a
car,
I cry and grieve for people that are still alive,
I always wonder how I can strengthen my
relationship with God?

I choose my outfits according to the time I will
be walking home,
I get baby fever often, but then I'm reminded of
that girl with the list.
Never liked cheese and onion crisps, they make
your breath stink.
I still say thank you to the driver,
I love Black Men but I will not be the one to
help you through the storm, I need to save and
heal myself.

Maybe I was a bit rash cutting off that
friendship, but at least I don't have to worry
about surprise parties,
I feel the need to change my hair all the time,
60% of the time I feel sh*t but say I'm fine,

Which is hypocritical of me to say because I'll
make sure everyone's mental health is okay
except mine.

Why is heterosexual sex normal in a
conversation, but a mention of a vagina and all
hell breaks loose ?
Men getting emotional over football makes me
laugh,
I worry about all the black and brown missing
children that are not on the news.

I get jealous of people who have traveled a lot,
because I'm constantly thinking, would it be
safe for me ?
Despite growing up in London, I still love South
the most ,
not the artisan coffee shops in Peckham ,
(coffee is actually disgusting)
I'm talking 3 for £1 plantain,
and Aunty is asking if you need your hair done.

I wish I asked how you felt, even if I didn't like
the answer.
I've definitely sent a picture of him to my sister
and said he looks better in real life.
I secretly watch his stories on insta stories.

I still think about Stephen Lawerence,

I'm at my happiest when I'm in Jamaica,
I want to love in bold letters.

Why Primark isn't online is ruthless, I want a
pack of socks and a Lady has a shopping basket
for her family of four.
Movies were so much better when they were on
CDs,
My love language is me cussing someone out,
it's a defense mechanism (a bit toxic init),
I love watching crime documentaries when I'm
doing my makeup.

I was always amazed at how a Teacher had time
to beef a teenager.

Why aren't sanitary products free ?
Also if you buy more fruits and vegetables, how
can they be nutritious if they're not in season and
genetically modified ?
If they brought back CBBC, I would binge
watch all the shows.
If you're in the UK and need a conversation
starter, talk about the weather.

Kettle

We bought a kettle together,
the one where it matches the colour scheme of
the kitchen.
Blends in but holds significance,
proud in its structure as it stands in solidarity.

Made cups of tea for me and you,
Time and time again,
But when would you fill up the kettle ?
I'm getting extremely tired of constantly
filling it up myself.

I let it go after a while,
And I continued.
Family and friends complemented its
Lively, funny and loving appearance.
They said I was lucky and wished
to have one like mine.
If they looked inside they would think
otherwise.

Months went by and I'd had enough.

I was tired of filling the kettle all the way,
and your inconsistent excuses for your delay.
Your deceitful character put on a play,
As you poured tea for others while they were
around,
This was now a circus because I became a
clown.

I stopped giving you tea,
And you delicately showered me in vile insults,
Protesting that I was selfish and lazy.
We sat on the swing going back and forth,
Until we talked it out ,
So I thought we came to a compromise.

Finally! You filled up the kettle,
but you came back with one cup.
You weren't sure if I wanted one, so I never
made a fuss.
You left me water in the kettle.
So I went to make myself some tea,
And the kettle was not even 10% filled.

So I must accept the limescale water that you
have left me.
I opened the cupboard to look for limescale
remover,

Only to find another kettle.
Very much used, where you had been filling it
up all the way from the start.

Salad

I love tomatoes, but not in a salad
I feel like sometimes it's too watery, and when it
gets mushy it ruins the consistency of salad.
Strawberries don't taste as good as they look,
similar to dragon fruit.
Walkers seriously need to bring back barbecue
crisps.

I'll never forget when I was 13 and my Dad gave
me $100 Jamaican Dollars and I thought I was
rich.
It was the equivalent to 54p.
Sometimes I really want a morning routine that
is so aesthetic, but even if I want to make a
smoothie bowl, I'm not blending frozen fruits at
7am,
 I would rather get more sleep.

I've never really been into the clubbing scene in
London, but Mayfair clubs not allowing mela-in
is very outlandish.
My mum still discourages me from wearing
braids to an interview and I know why.
I'm for interracial relationships, but as soon as I
hear
'I've never been with a black girl before', finito.
First of all I'm a Woman, so I don't know who
you're referring to, but secondly, what was the
need?

The stops on many bus routes are genuinely
ridiculous, it's at least a 3 minute walk between
them.
In 2019 I was going through trials and
tribulations, and I lost my phone at Victoria
Station and a bus driver messaged me on
Facebook and sent it to my address.
Gratitude is not even the word!

To tell women and men that domestic violence is
immoral, to then say that physical discipline in
childhood is necessary is very hypocritical. I'll
forever be grateful for watching Murdered by
My Boyfriend in school. It was so good that
anytime I saw him act in other movies or series,
I couldn't forget how he killed the mother of his
child.

I love British sitcoms probably because of the
familiarity.
I'm still upset with the finale of Line of Duty!
Will I ever know what happened on the fishing
trip?
If Lee and Lucy got married after 7 years of
friendship, was he always in the friend-zone?

I always ask men what football team they
support.
I'm nosy.
Sometimes stalking is very necessary,
I once found out a guy practiced Voodoo, I love
my Caribbeans but despite him being Haitian I
was not about to mess with my Salvation.
Why don't men like being called cute?
I pay very close attention to how a Man treats
children and animals.
How does a man that has a gel that can wash
their face, hair, body and still have clear skin?
I breakout when I've missed a step in my skin
care routine.

Move

31

History should not hold you captive, for you will
be unable to gain the fruits of the future.

Difference

I'm aware that my European Surname gets me interviews, and that me being the only black person means companies can tick the diversity box.
But do you allow locs? Is it too messy for your grooming standards ? Are cornrows too urban or eccentric for you? Is my afro exceptional? Because Angela Davies performed speeches with her crown of glory and she is more than professional.
You want the black face but not the person who takes up the space.
How does a difference of opinion equate to me being aggressive?
I found it excessive that a colleague messaged me that he 'had tried a black girl at a party before.' I was unaware that we were on the menu.
I pretend to not be bothered, because that's what I'm used to.
I was on the topic of dating and a colleague suggested that I should date a white man to have 'cappuccino babies', I felt so objectified.

These are all seen as innocent jokes, that are
light-hearted and I giggle because I carry my
pain in laughter.

It's Okay

Roses, daisies, smiles, blue skies everything was going just fine.
Until I cried. You'd think it's over something major.
Instead just a minor inconvenience.
But I didn't have time for this poor-small-me act, I've been doing independent Black Superhero Woman, for sometime now.
I was at your beck and call when you needed me, I'd pull up to any scenery.
It still hurts because you still mistreated me.
Present but it feels like you're miles away, and therefore I felt alone.
I was screaming right in front of you and you still didn't know, or maybe you didn't care.

If I had a flower for every time I cried, I'd be the owner of Holland Park.

That's where I often went when I was in the
dark.
Something about natural scenery refreshes me,
it's as if I surround myself in it.
It gave me peace of mind.

So it is not about the fact that I cried today, but
the memories it brought back.
I must remember that strong-minded people
were once weak so it is okay if at times I feel
Meek.

A blur

Black Girl Magic, that's what they say,
So why am I taking it day by day?
Sometimes I was barely stable but you'd still see
me in the function,
caressed in the fluorescent lights and its
humidity.
I'd lose myself, I have my girls and it's fine
because they will always find a way back to me,
becoming best friends with the girls in the toilet,
oversharing because we had shit to deal with, so
I'd dance away in escapades hoping to feel
something,
because intimacy doesn't necessarily mean that
you're into me, but I'd learnt that way too late.
So Wray makes me decline your call because it's
easy, but just want you to come and see me but
for what?
Because closure is just a new introduction of a
new chapter,
so I loved you more in my head rather than what
I saw with my eyes instead.

Looking at star signs to see their compatibility,
which is silly because if you're not a Christian
I'II just cross you out without a doubt.
Why did I drag it out so long?
When you just used to drag me down.
Covid had my mind in disarray and I'd definitely
shed more than three tears, making more dumb
decisions, so I guess Channah lost and Ella Won,
but your plight is no longer my fight no more.

Pollock

I'm a bit of a mess,
I'm not going to pretend that I have it together
because I'd be lying,
And then I'd have to call myself Boris, And tbh
I'm constantly thinking of ways of how to add
extra zeros to my salary.
I wanna lose weight but burn counting calories.
Because then there will be no soul in the food.
I stress over the kind of music I listen to, they
say separate the art from the the artist, but how
can I sing that somebody is now heartless,
When did songs become a CV of the lives that
have been taken?
Am I contributing to this madness all for the
sake of a beat?
My mind races through many thoughts a day, I
wish I knew the formula but I know it's not one.
There is so much I want to say but I just resort to
silence.
Half of the battle is in your mind
I believe in going forth and multiplying.

But I'm a black woman and I guess we see
hospitals the same way black men see police
stations.
Will we ever make it out?
I don't like talking about love because we're in a
constant battle, but justice was never served so I
guess we never MET. I will know I have found
love when it feels like poetry.

A Trail of thoughts

I still remember the day I found out Micheal
Jackson died, that's all me and my friends would
talk about that day.
I sometimes felt distant from my friends because
I was secluded from certain activities.
I used to often lie and say my mum said no, but I
just assumed so, because the idea of sleeping
somewhere else when I had a bed was dunce.
In secondary school, Paul's Boutique was in and
it felt like everyone had one except me.
2015 had me in a chokehold with Drill music as
I sat at the back of the bus twiddling with my
headphone wires trying to get the other ear to
work.

Which is weird because I don't wear headphones
if I'm in a dark or secluded area.

I always analyze the way in which I speak to
men so that I don't give off the wrong signals.
Try not to be too nice or too blunt.
When I say no to men's advances I feel like
Goliath, but that is shortly followed up by
feeling like a mouse, as I can't control how men
handle rejection.

I don't know what I miss more, the bendy bus or
paying a cash fare.
I never bring personal issues to light in public
because it can end up on shadeborough.
When people mention Stratford, I still reminisce
when videos were made by teens asking 'Team
Lightskin or Darkskin'.
Black on Black Crime is just a scapegoat term.

I remember my colleague walking me home at
11pm after Rashford, Sancho and Saka missed
their penalties.

I still want to learn the offside rule and be able
to spot it during a game.
I want to sit on a swing in Bali.
I want to conferences with David Lammy or
Akala.
I spend time with someone and I love the
moment, but remember that it will come to an
end and I'm overwhelmed by sadness.

A mango should only be eaten if it looks like a
relaxed Mohican after.
As a nation are we ever going to find out what
happened to Madeline McCann ?

I probably shouldn't have replied to that text at
2am, especially when I said it's the last time.
I'll never stop talking about love. It's never
ending.

Surrender

I sit back and look at how we navigate within
the world,
how I take my place and where I fit in,
and when I feel overwhelmed I remember,
The Lord says 'lean not on your own
understanding.'

I constantly find myself in the rat race,
so I guess I'm always chasing bread,
but I should really be receiving the one at the
altar instead.

It gets to me that people idolize celebrities,
who's hot, who's not,
scaling them on levels they can't even reach,
because if you can't teach good values then what
use are you to me?

I'm not surprised when a sinner acts cynical.
I know a few that sit in the pew,
a wolf in sheep's clothing,
smiling at your blessings but deep down they are
really loathing.

I want better for my people, especially the young
black boys,
you should carry your boy on your back and not
your shoulder,
that weight is too heavy for you to carry.
I care about your life and I don't want to see you
on either end of a knife.

You have a purpose and vision.
So fly high but never get birded, my word is the
burden is always too heavy to bear.

A quiet exit

45

Love snuck out the back door